Du même auteur

chez Gulf Stream Éditeur

La Corderie royale
Ces drôles d'oiseaux sur le chantier de l'Hermione

chez M6 Éditions

À la recherche du dinosaure géant, coll. « Max la science »

dans la collection « Mes drôles de questions sur », dirigée par Mac Lesggy

La Vie quotidienne
Le Corps humain
Les Animaux sauvages
L'Histoire de France
La Terre
Les Chiens et les chats

© Gulf Stream Éditeur, Saint-Herblain 2011
ISBN : 978-2-35488-143-6
Loi 49-956 du 16 juillet 1949 sur les publications destinées à la jeunesse

Texts and illustrations by

Didier Georget

crróak

LIFE ABOARD

THE FRIGATE

HERMIONE

Lafayette's frigate

English translation by

Catherine Le Calvé

Gulf Stream Éditeur

Contents

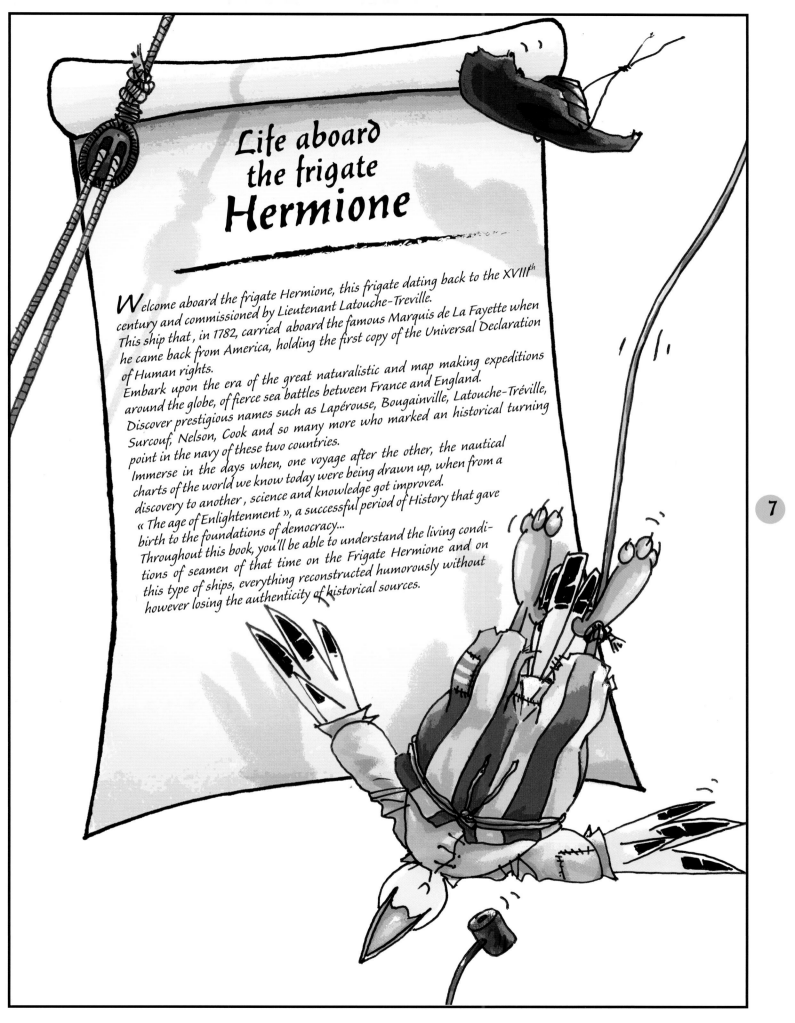

Life aboard the frigate Hermione

Welcome aboard the frigate Hermione, this frigate dating back to the XVIIIth century and commissioned by Lieutenant Latouche-Treville. This ship that, in 1782, carried aboard the famous Marquis de La Fayette when he came back from America, holding the first copy of the Universal Declaration of Human rights.

Embark upon the era of the great naturalistic and map making expeditions around the globe, of fierce sea battles between France and England. Discover prestigious names such as Lapérouse, Bougainville, Latouche-Tréville, Surcouf, Nelson, Cook and so many more who marked an historical turning point in the navy of these two countries.

Immerse in the days when, one voyage after the other, the nautical charts of the world we know today were being drawn up, when from a discovery to another, science and knowledge got improved.

« The age of Enlightenment », a successful period of History that gave birth to the foundations of democracy...

Throughout this book, you'll be able to understand the living conditions of seamen of that time on the Frigate Hermione and on this type of ships, everything reconstructed humorously without however losing the authenticity of historical sources.

In those days, living as a seaman was hardly enviable. Life aboard warships or big merchant ships was very hard, comfort was missing, body hygiene was at its simplest, seamen's food diet was drastic and their work was very painful. When they were at sea, working conditions got harder in case of heavy weather and when added to the harshness of everyday, would decimate the sickest ones one by one.

Taken on board from an early age, the boys escaped from childhood and violently moved into the adult world.

No special treatment on board. The topman, the ordinary seaman, the carpenter or the cook, each position was a vital link in the chain that ensured the smooth operation of these ships. It was out of the question to fail in your duty or you may have been punished! Vessels or frigates, carrying from 300 to more than 600 men: these ones were genuine onboard garrisons that had to be controlled, everyone's mood was so changing, depending on whether it was windy or not and on epidemic diseases.

The hierarchy on board didn't tolerate any favour and mutiny remained for the captain, the only master in command of the ship, the biggest danger. Disciplin and justice turned out to be the only means to counter this heresy.

Cruises, which often lasted several months, caused a considerable amount of casualties.

The big blue, as the scene of battles, of ship chases, of boardings, of discoveries, and of many shipwrecks, has remained for man all throughout History a very important place of education. Fair wind and following seas...

Longitudinal section of the frigate

Gun deck
Main capstern
Hood of the main ladder
Gangwa
ladder
Poultry cages
Quarter deck
Wheelhouse-steering
wheel, rudder control
Poop
Headquarters
Naval officers's cabins
Stores hatchway
COT COT COT!
Council room
Captain's cabin
Master Gunner's cabin
Gun room
Grain locker
Biscuit locker
Magazine
Steward's room
Gunpowder keg bunker
The hold for the Captain's food supplies
He fed the members of the staff captain at his table
Wine hold
Oil and vinegar hold
Bread oven
Cannonb
pitt

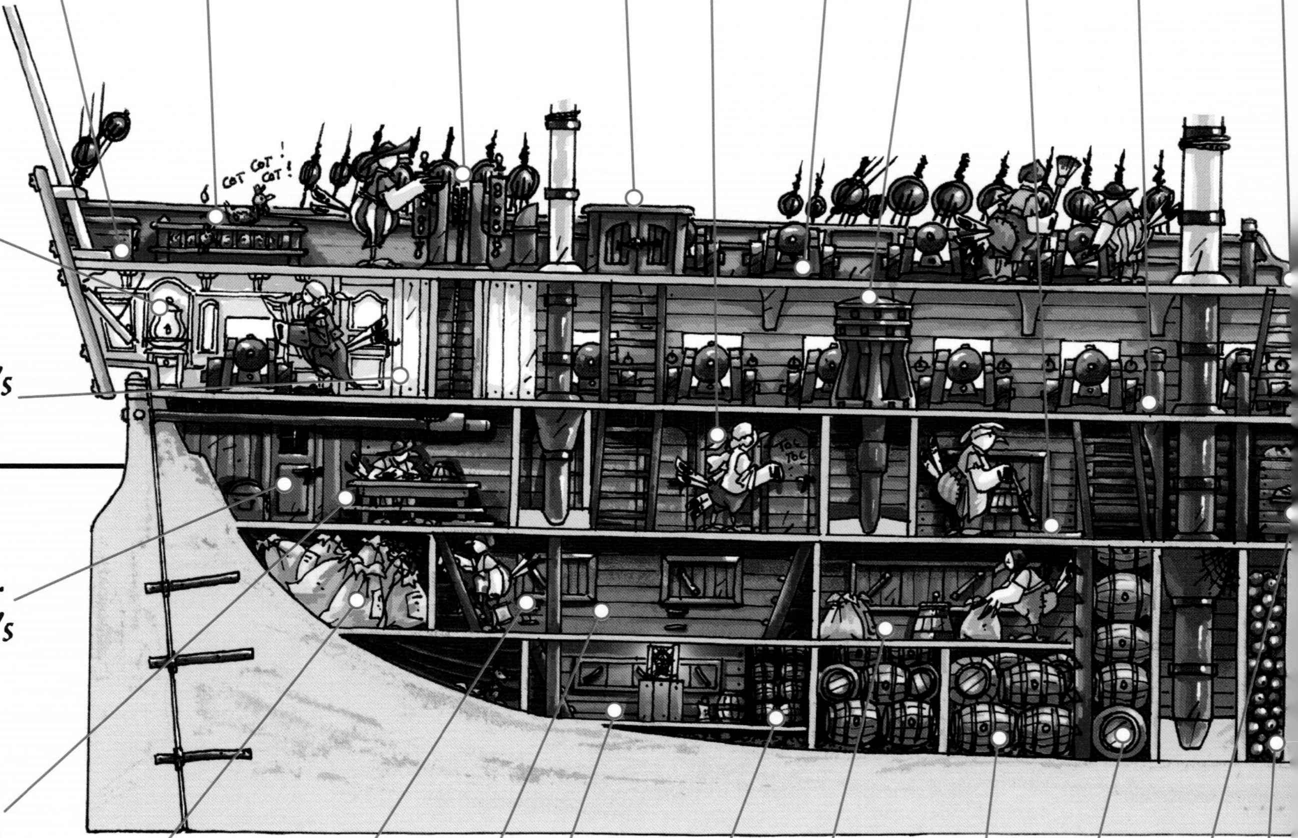

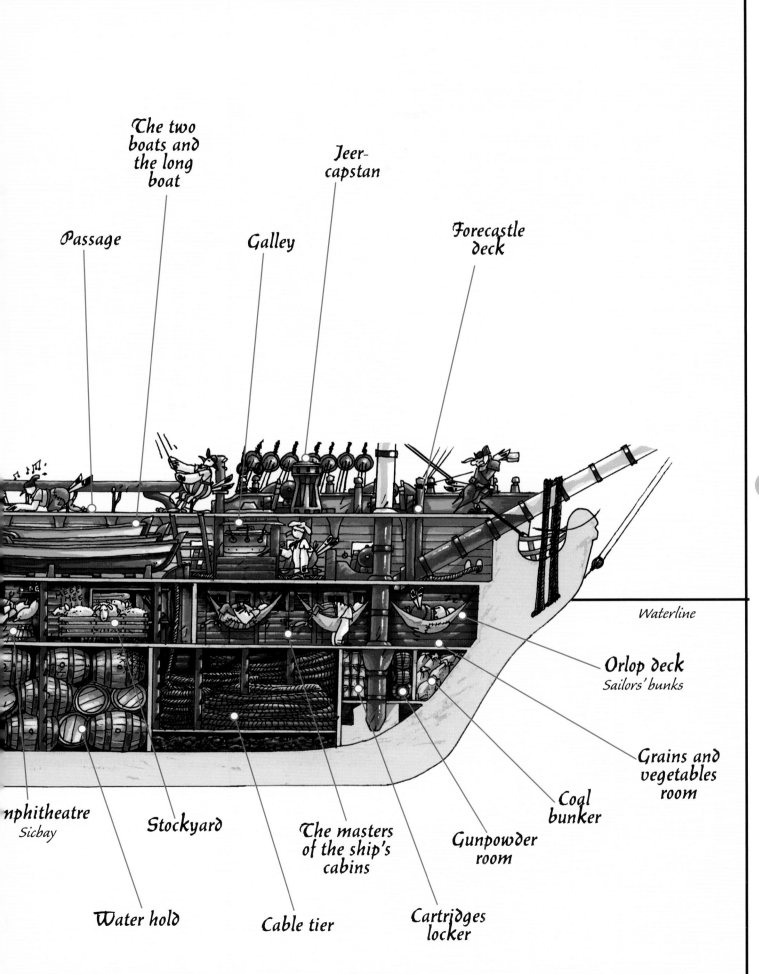

The two
boats and
the long
boat

Jeer-
capstan

Passage

Galley

Forecastle
deck

11

Waterline

Orlop deck
Sailors' bunks

Grains and
vegetables
room

Coal
bunker

mphitheatre
Sicbay

Stockyard

The masters
of the ship's
cabins

Gunpowder
room

Water hold

Cable tier

Cartridges
locker

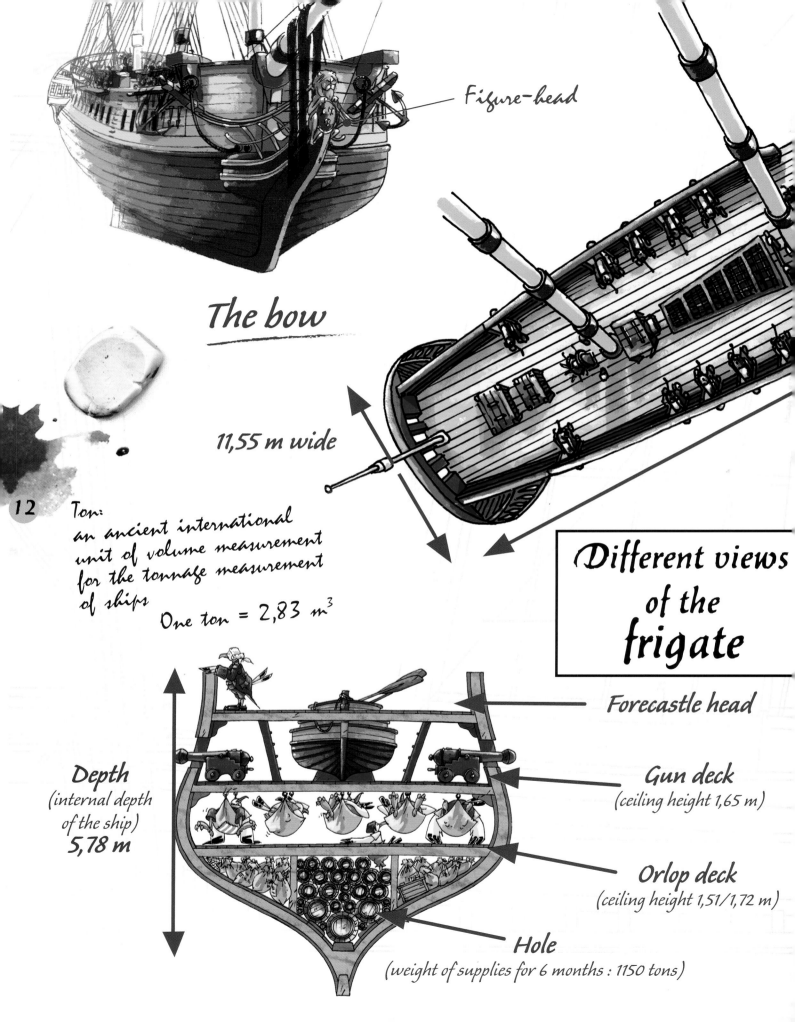

Figure-head

The bow

11,55 m wide

12

Ton:
an ancient international unit of volume measurement for the tonnage measurement of ships

One ton = 2,83 m³

Different views of the **frigate**

Forecastle head

Gun deck
(ceiling height 1,65 m)

Orlop deck
(ceiling height 1,51/1,72 m)

Hole
(weight of supplies for 6 months : 1150 tons)

Depth
(internal depth of the ship)
5,78 m

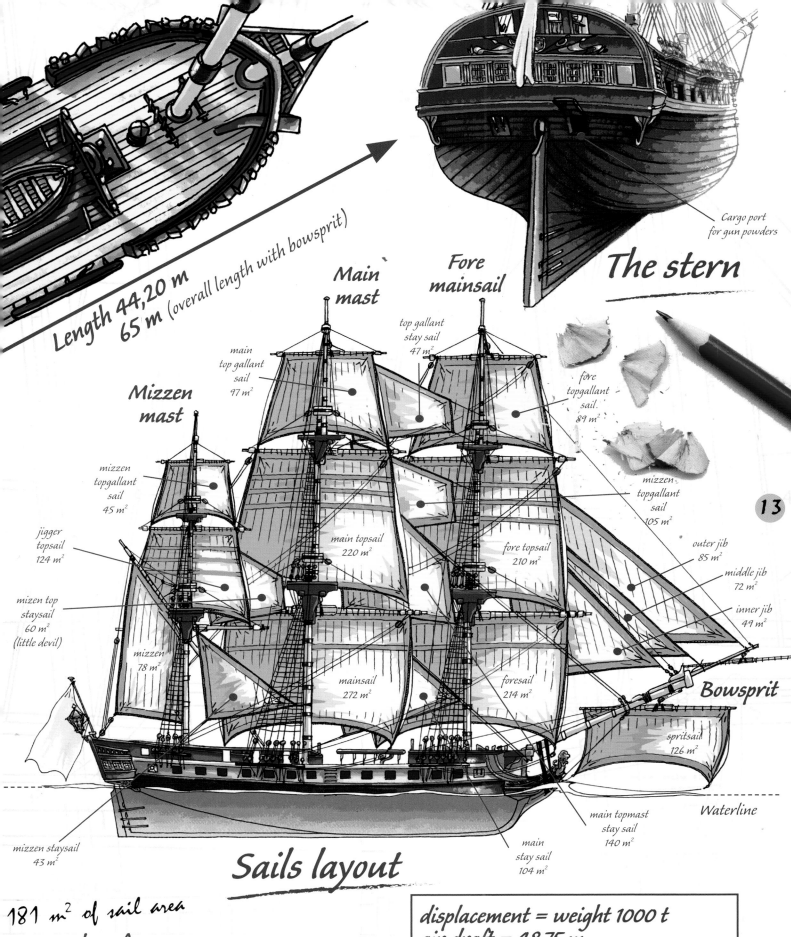

Length 44,20 m
65 m (overall length with bowsprit)

Main mast

Fore mainsail

Cargo port for gun powders

The stern

Mizzen mast

main top gallant sail 97 m²

top gallant stay sail 47 m²

fore topgallant sail. 89 m²

mizzen topgallant sail 45 m²

mizzen topgallant sail 105 m²

13

jigger topsail 124 m²

main topsail 220 m²

fore topsail 210 m²

outer jib 85 m²

middle jib 72 m²

mizen top staysail 60 m² (little devil)

inner jib 49 m²

mizzen 78 m²

mainsail 272 m²

foresail 214 m²

Bowsprit

spritsail 126 m²

mizzen staysail 43 m²

main topmast stay sail 140 m²

Waterline

Sails layout

main stay sail 104 m²

181 m² of sail area

27 km of rope
+ 5 km sapre
130 to 140 t of ballast

displacement = weight 1000 t
air draft = 48,75 m
(from waterline to the top of the mast)
draft = 5,68 m

The stores loaded in the bunkers and in the holds were usually calculated for a 6-month period. So, the belly of the ship was filled with supplies and various things, with small or big spare equipment for the fittings, the sails and the rope, with ordnance, gunshots and gunpowder, with perishable food products preserved in salt as best as can be expected, in order to face up to the insalubrity that reigns, with livestock, all kinds of liquids such as water, wine, alcohol, oil, vinegar...
When all these things were displayed on the dock before loading, it was hard to believe that they could fit in the belly of these ships. In that damp obscurity, the main difficulty remained the preservation of fresh water. It could hardly last more than a month. As it stagnated, it was bedecked with repulsive colours and emitted a strong putrid smell. Quickly, worms and other bacteria were joining up.
It was a fertile ground for diseases...

A list of equipement and supplies
on board of a 12 pounder class frigate for 6 months

Equipment		Supplies	
Arms & Ordnance		Water	84 000 litres
		Wine	39 708 litres
		Tafia	600 litres
		Olive oil	1000 litres
		Vinegar	550 litres
12-pound cannonball	1500.-		
Bar shot	1500.-	Salt	1200 kilos
Cartridge of a canon	3000.-	Sugar	150 kilos
Bullet bag	60.-	Flour	10 000 kilos
		Biscuits	30630 kilos
Gunpowder	10 tonnes	Cod-fish	187 kilos
		Cheese	873 kilos
		Bacon	5405 kilos
12-pound cannon	26.-	Beef	974 kilos
6-pound cannon	6.-	Vegetables	4480 kilos
	10.-	Rice	1698 kilos
	4.-	Charcoal	1000 kil

Packing supplies

Bundles of kindling : used for wedging the barrels altogether and for feeding the fire for the cook's kitchen.

* (Swaths)

Barrel	Half hogshead	Quarter of a barrel for flour	Quarter of a barrel for bacon meat fish	15-buckets barrel vinegar olive oil	Water-cask gunpowder
242 l	121 l	60,5 l			

To preserve water, the barrels were "rinced out": they were rinsed out with pure lime water until a protective skin appeared on the inner surface which could help preserving its clearness a little longer.

Peas Fava beans — Rice — Biscuits — Charcoal

Yum yum !!

Material onboard was elaborately ordered according to accurat stowage plans.

Powder barrel to carry gunpowder — Bucket pump to evacuate water from the ship

The yard :

It was the rigorous way the rows of barrels (hogsheads) were compartmentalized, carefully stacked and solidly tied up so that the access to the lower levels became organized and safe. The equilibrium of the frigate depended on these goods and on the weight distribution among the holds and the bunkers. Each hogshead and each cask that were emptied had to be systematically filled with saltwater. A ship could not tolerate any mess.

Weights - measures - capacities...

Liquids :

A chopine : 0,46 l = 1/2 pint

A pint : 0,93 l

A demijohn (carboy) used to carry wine and alcohol to the staff captain's table : from 14,25 l to 19 l = 15 to 20 pints

A pot : 1,9 l = 2 pints

Currency :

Sol : 1 sol = 12 deniers

Masses :

1 pound : 16 ounces = 489 g

1 ounce : 8 drams = 30,50 g

1 dram : 3,8 g

For grains :

1 bushel : 13 l

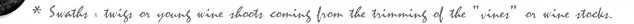

Hierarchy
of the ships and of the crew

A ship-of-the-line

3 gun decks

Warship

Difficult to handle
Strong firepower

74 to 118 gun barrels
600 to 800 men

A frigate
same as the Hermione

1 gun deck

Escort boat

Faster then a vessel,
used as a patrol-vessel

24 to 30 gun barrels
300 men

A fluyt

1 huge hold

Transport ship

Few arms,
few men,
carrying the goods

A small
fishing vessel

1 fish hold

Fishing boat

Few arms,
few men,
fishing off
the Atlantic coast

Carton 119, N: 13.

Ship's log

On the ship's log, the captain recorded hour after hour, day after day, each maneuver, each slightest action or gesture of importance. It was the only written record of the cruise and the only official account, if need be, for the royal courts of justice back home...

croack !!

More than 300 men aboard !

The reputation of a ship depended on the captain's own reputation and every seaman knew how important it was before reporting for duty. Whatever his rank was, his bravery and his victories were enough to maintain discipline. Many seamen travelled all around the seas bearing the colours of the Royal Navy or their own, they were, above all, adventurers...

The Captain

The only master of the ship after God...

The staff-captain
14 people

Officers,
an almoner,
a surgeon,
an apothecary...

The masters of the ship
44 people

Master carpenter,
master caulker,
boatswain,
master gunner,
master blacksmith,
master sail maker...

The soldiers of the frigate's garrison
35 people

Soldiers,
non-commissioned
officers...

The Supernumeraries
(staff which was not directly connected to the marine corps)
71 people

The messboy,
the butcher,
the baker,
the cook,
the cabin boys...

The seamen
152 people
12 topmen, 9 steersmen, 131 sailors

The shipboys
31 children

Wind astern

Port Broad reach

Broad Starboard reach

Port reach

Starboard reach

Close Starboard reach

Port close reach

Wind direction

Port close hauled

Starboard close hauled

Tacking
tacking close-hauled to the wind in order to come round.

Speed

Close-hauled : from 9 to 11 knots = 20 km/h
Beam reach : From 15 to 16 knots = 37 km/h
Wind astern : from 10 to 11 knots = 20 km/h

Head to wind :
nose to the wind.

Slackening the sail :
give slack.

*Tacking :
tack against the wind.

Hauling in the sheet :
on the contrary, heaving tight.

*Jibing

*Jibing :
formerly windward side from the back : changing tack with the wind astern.

*Luffing :
tack in order to get closer to the wind.

*Luffing

Luffing

*Falling off the wind :
opposite of luffing, changing tack to keep away from the eye of the wind.

Headwind zone

*Falling off the wind

Starboard tack :
receiving the wind by starboard.

*Tacking

Port tack :
receiving the wind by portside

The wind

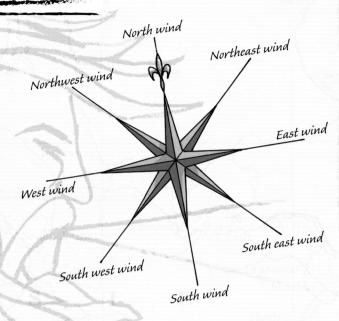

North wind
Northeast wind
Northwest wind
East wind
West wind
South east wind
South west wind
South wind

SEA STATE

Force	Description	Height in metre
0	glassy	0
1	rippled	0 to 0,1
2	smooth	0,1 to 0,5
3	slight	0,5 to 1,25
4	moderate	1,25 to 2,25
5	rough	2,5 to 4
6	very rough	4 to 6
7	high	6 to 9
8	very high	9 to 14
9	phenomenal	14 and over

WIND STRENGTH

Speed in km/h	Name
0	calm
4	light air
9	light breeze
11	gentle breeze
14	moderate breeze
22	fresh breeze
29	strong breeze
36	moderate gale
43	fresh gale
54	strong gale
72	whole gale - storm
144	hurricane

Meteorology

Sayings

Meteorology is not an exact science, and at that time,
for lack of daily weather forecasts of which today's sailors
can take advantage, you only had to rely on yourself.
Seasoned sailors passed on their precious skills
in the form of sayings, not always reliable.
But for their defenses, today's meteorology is not always foolproof...

Haloes around the sun or moon indicate a rain or snow real soon.

A wind from the south has rain in its mouth

When the sun sets bright and clear, an easterly wind you need not fear.

Red sky in the morning, sailor take warning.

The heel

The ship's angle of heel couldn't exceed 20° degrees, at open ports.

20°   20°

Heaving

When there was a storm, using a smaller sail to the maximum, keeping only one course (low sail), luffing closed-hauled so as to keep steering and to be able to face the waves.

Time on board

Time is calculated using hourglasses of varying durations : 60, 30, 15 mn...
On board, time is determined with hourglasses that are turned without interruption since the beginning of the journey.

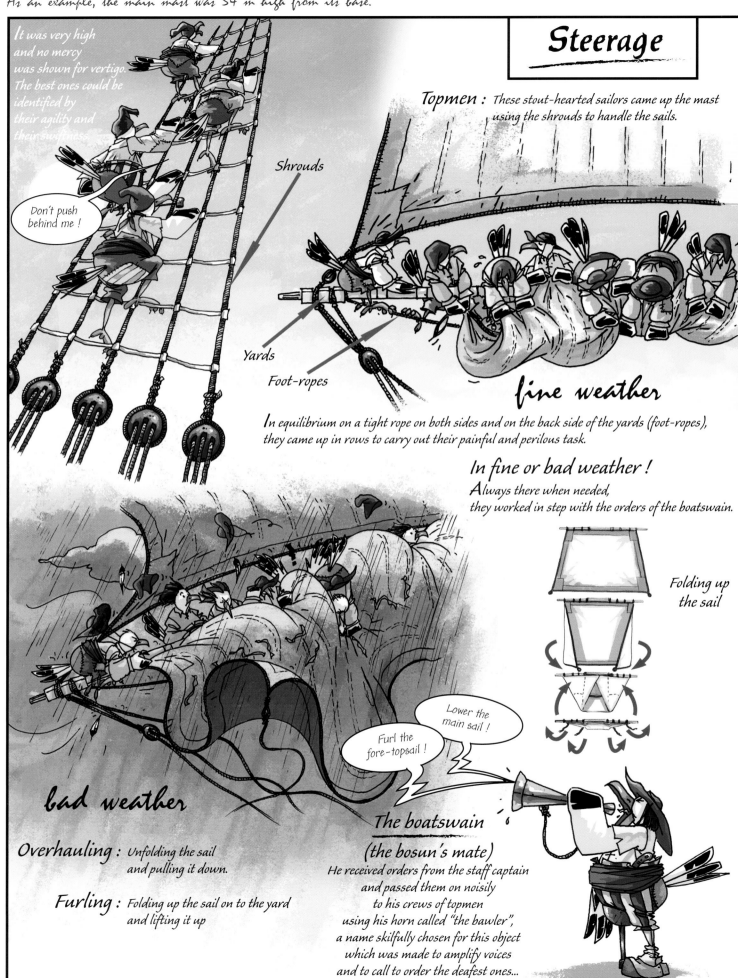

Steerage

It was very high and no mercy was shown for vertigo. The best ones could be identified by their agility and their swiftness.

Don't push behind me !

Shrouds

Yards

Foot-ropes

Topmen : These stout-hearted sailors came up the mast using the shrouds to handle the sails.

fine weather

In equilibrium on a tight rope on both sides and on the back side of the yards (foot-ropes), they came up in rows to carry out their painful and perilous task.

In fine or bad weather !
Always there when needed, they worked in step with the orders of the boatswain.

Folding up the sail

Lower the main sail !

Furl the fore-topsail !

bad weather

Overhauling : Unfolding the sail and pulling it down.

Furling : Folding up the sail on to the yard and lifting it up

The boatswain

(the bosun's mate)
He received orders from the staff captain and passed them on noisily to his crews of topmen using his horn called "the bawler", a name skilfully chosen for this object which was made to amplify voices and to call to order the deafest ones...

20

At the capstan

This was the only time when the men were allowed to sing to cheer themselves up, their work being so much arduous. These songs were bawdy and often vindictive to the captain. "Once is not always".

The capstan

Turning on itself with the force of its arms, the big one at the back of the orlop-deck enabled to lift up the anchor, and the small one located on the forecastle, to pull down or to hoist the lower yards.

The wheelhouse

It was the place where you could find the control house : the helm that activated the rudder.
The master kept a very watchful eye on his compass and on his course, whatever the sea conditions.
A crew with a second pilot and his pilot's mates was there to take turns and to make sure that they didn't wander off the course dictated by the captain.

The lifeline

It was a rope that was tightened from one side of the ship to the other in stress of weather.
It helped the men, shaken by the swell and by the stray, to keep their balance while they were moving.
Men could not stop working on a frigate, day or night...

The waist anchor

4,5 t

9 doughty strong fellows to handle a cannon...

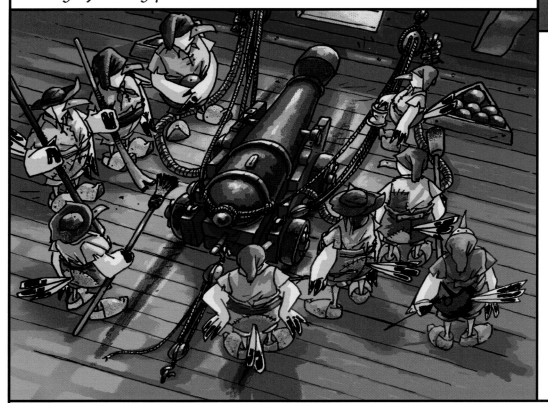

32 cannons on board
that is to say :
26 12-pound cannons
6 6-pound cannons

Not less than 9 men
were required to manoeuvre
this centerpiece of
the shipboard ordnance,
weighing more than 2 t
and very tricky to handle
because of the gunpowder
it contained.
When the work pace
was at its maximum,
a gun could be fired
every five minutes,
all that being done
in a very small space.

Bold men cleaning gunpowder residues with a go-devil after each firing...

What a filth !

Husky men putting the cannon in its right axis...

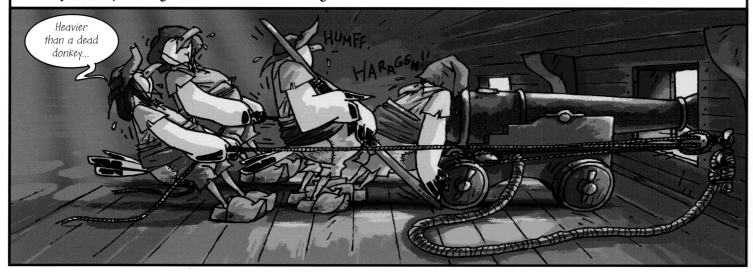

Heavier than a dead donkey...

HUMFF, HARRGGN!!

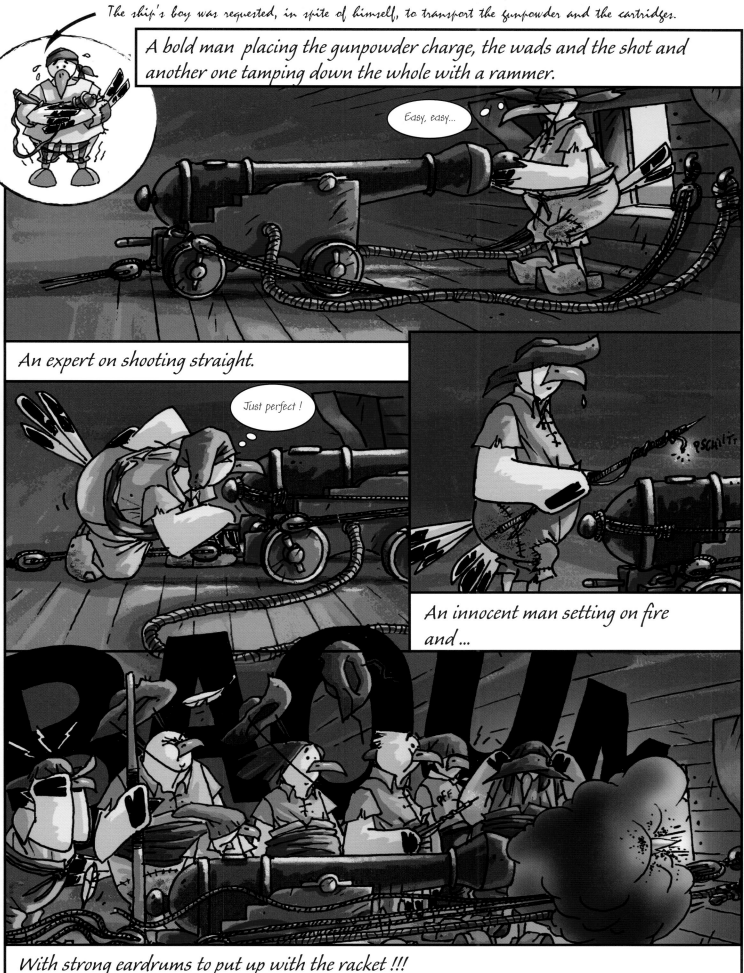

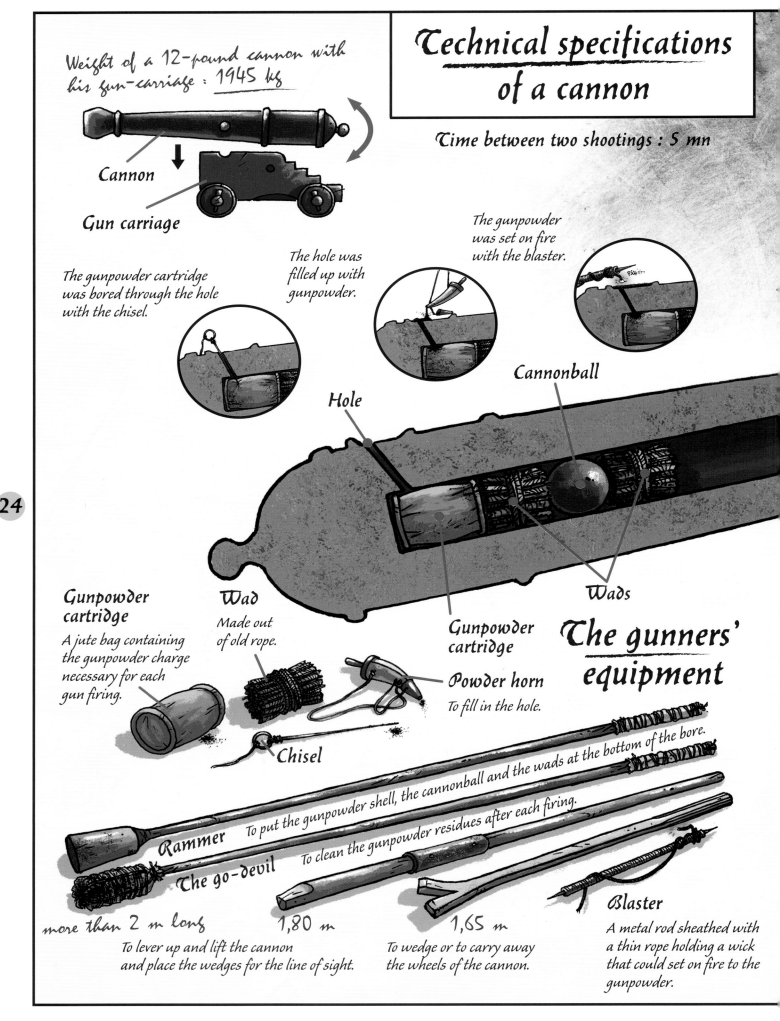

Weight of a 12-pound cannon with his gun-carriage : **1945 kg**

Cannon

Gun carriage

Time between two shootings : 5 mn

The gunpowder cartridge was bored through the hole with the chisel.

The hole was filled up with gunpowder.

The gunpowder was set on fire with the blaster.

PSCHITT

Cannonball

Hole

Wads

Gunpowder cartridge

A jute bag containing the gunpowder charge necessary for each gun firing.

Wad

Made out of old rope.

Gunpowder cartridge

Powder horn

To fill in the hole.

Chisel

The gunners' equipment

Rammer To put the gunpowder shell, the cannonball and the wads at the bottom of the bore.

The go-devil To clean the gunpowder residues after each firing.

more than 2 m long

To lever up and lift the cannon and place the wedges for the line of sight.

1,80 m

1,65 m

To wedge or to carry away the wheels of the cannon.

Blaster

A metal rod sheathed with a thin rope holding a wick that could set on fire to the gunpowder.

24

Different calibres of cannons

Sound comparable to 180 Db = lift-off of a rocket.

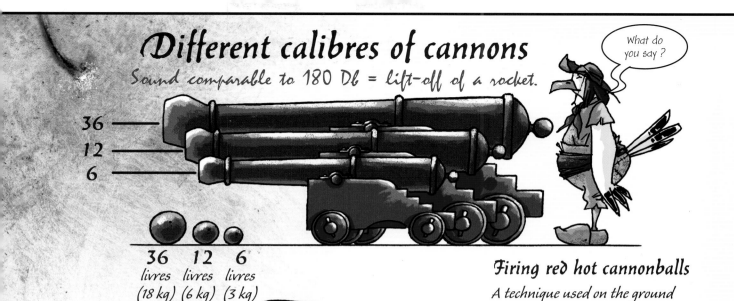

What do you say?

36
12
6

36 livres (18 kg) 12 livres (6 kg) 6 livres (3 kg)

Broadside

A set of cannons located at one side of the ship, "fire of a broadside".

Firing red hot cannonballs

A technique used on the ground and that consisted in making the cannonballs red hot in an oven so that they became incendiary.

The bore of the cannon

Different types of firing

One foot : 33 cm

Maximum firing range on the ground : 600 feet = 300 m
Maximum firing range at sea so as to be effective, not more than 180 feet = 60m

Wedges for the line of sight

Made in wood and of differents sizes, they enabled to adjust the firing height of the cannon.

Cannonball	**"Round shot"** fire aimed at damaging the hulls of the ships with repeated shootings, and sometimes at making them sink.	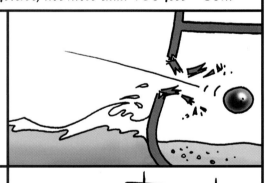
Two headed bar shot	**"Dismasting fire"** fire aiming at dismasting the ships with the help of projectiles twirling in the air and that violently hit the masting. A dismasted ship is a ship brought to a standstill.	CRACK!!
Grapeshot 	**"Raking fire"** fire aiming at causing as many damages among the crew as possible with the help of this projectile filled up with lead shot. (metal slashed into a multitude of small specks).	AïE OUïLLE!! AïE!! 

Technical specifications of great guns

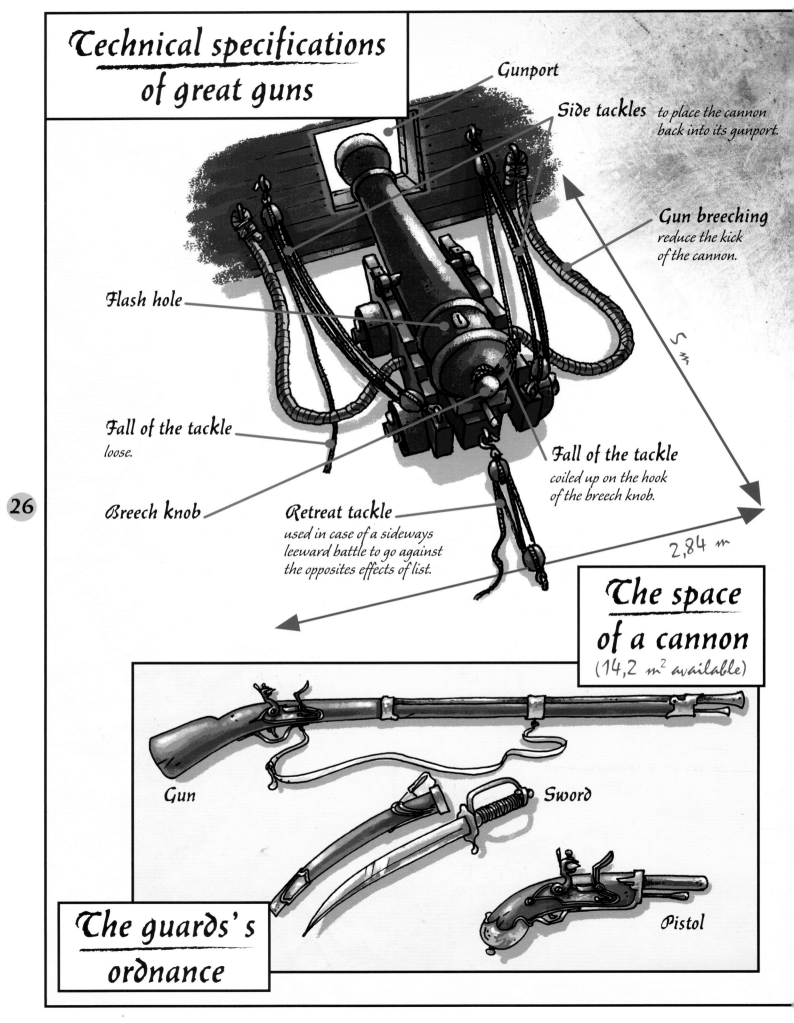

Gunport

Side tackles *to place the cannon back into its gunport.*

Gun breeching *reduce the kick of the cannon.*

Flash hole

Fall of the tackle *loose.*

Breech knob

Retreat tackle *used in case of a sideways leeward battle to go against the opposites effects of list.*

Fall of the tackle *coiled up on the hook of the breech knob.*

5 m

2,84 m

The space of a cannon
(14,2 m² available)

The guards's ordnance

Gun

Sword

Pistol

How to reload firearms...

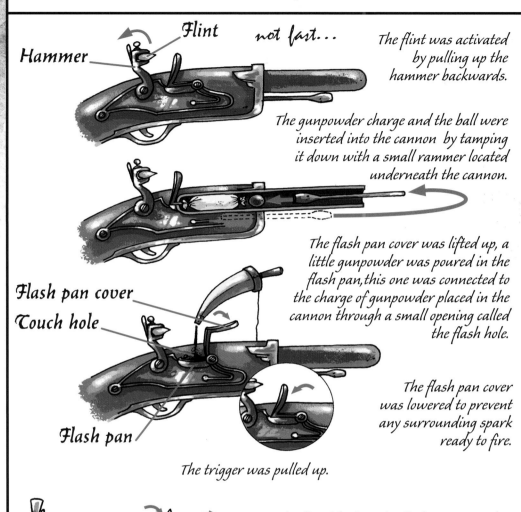

Hammer

Flint

not fast...

The flint was activated by pulling up the hammer backwards.

The gunpowder charge and the ball were inserted into the cannon by tamping it down with a small rammer located underneath the cannon.

Flash pan cover

Touch hole

The flash pan cover was lifted up, a little gunpowder was poured in the flash pan, this one was connected to the charge of gunpowder placed in the cannon through a small opening called the flash hole.

The flash pan cover was lowered to prevent any surrounding spark ready to fire.

Flash pan

The trigger was pulled up.

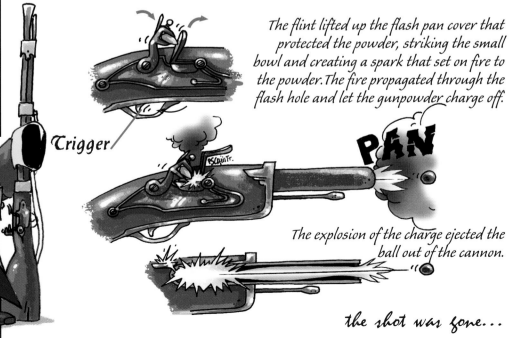

The flint lifted up the flash pan cover that protected the powder, striking the small bowl and creating a spark that set on fire to the powder. The fire propagated through the flash hole and let the gunpowder charge off.

Trigger

PAN

The explosion of the charge ejected the ball out of the cannon.

the shot was gone...

Naval battles

Naval battles, at that time, were dreadful. They took place amid a deafening din, a circle of light penetrating here and there through a nauseating and acrid thick smoke, and the men burning off bit by bit in a scorching heat. Clearly, the strike force of a 118-gun ship three deckers and the one of a 32-gun frigate were incommensurable. Intimidation was often enough to simmer down your enemy, but in case of the contrary, the warring party, in want of a shrewd strategy, would end by the board with a crash...

29

The surgeon

Bonesaw

Bullet puller

Screw tourniquet

Various knives

Hatchet and sledgehammer for the difficult bits.

In his den called the theatre, the surgeon and apothecary, a kind of one-man band, practised his art against the tide... As there was no hygiene and a lot of malnutrition, people died at sea more after infectious diseases than of fighting wounds.

Rhum or tafia universal anaesthetic

Flasks of miracle potions

Leather gag a braid made in leather that one had to bite in order to endure the pain of the surgical operation and to stop yelling.

Thread and needle to stitch up wounds.

The most common and devastating diseases on the ships contemporary of the Hermione were the scurvy, typhus fever, typhoid fever, smallpox and dysentery.
There was, most of the time, a fatal outcome, the main goal of the doctor was to avoid contagion at all costs. During theses times, many crews were decimated because of epidemics. Wounds became infected due to this bad hygiene, and generally, amputation came to be the only remedy.

Amputation

A tourniquet was applied before the limb to cut away, you cut...

①

Hot pitch* was poured on the wound for cauterization.

②

Once it was healed, a peg leg (the pilon, forerunner of today's artificial limbs) was custom made

③

Trepanning

Frequently used in case of violent shock at the head to treat bruises.

② Once the hole was drilled, the pus or the blood could then be extracted from the skull. The bruise was resorbed.

Drill bit

various bits

① First, a hole was drilled in the skull with the help of a drill bit, a type of breast drill, where the blow was striken...

③ Then a coin or a piece of metal was placed on it to obstruct the wound, the whole was protected by a bandage and the work was done...

④ Soon, chairs renewed themselves and bit by bit, the wound disappeared and changed into a simple scar.

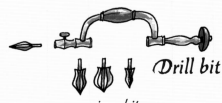

* Pitch : a type of tar that was used to coat the hulls of the ships to make them watertight.

30

Diseases on board

Seasickness
due to pitching and rolling.

Binge drinking
due to an abuse of tafia, that name (biture in French) was also given to the rope zigzagging through the deck.

The head
hit with a yard.

The head and the arm
hit with a yard and with a 12-pound round shot.

The head, the arm and the leg
fall of the shrouds...

Scurvy
a disease caused by a lack in vitamin C in the food (teeth fall, temperature, weakened state most of the time causing death)

Smallpox
an infectious disease, extremely contagious and fatal in 15 % of the cases.

bacillus

Typhoid fever
a disease caused by the bacteria found in water.

Dysentery
gastric infections causing painful and bloody diarrheas

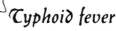

Yellow fever
caused by mosquito bites

Death
In extreme cases, the dead body was put in a canvas bag, sewn and ballasted, and after a short ceremony delivered by the chaplain on board, the deceased was thrown into the sea.

Typhus
due to dirtiness and spread by lice.

Some of them, without knowing it, protected themselves by eating rat. Rat's liver has a high level in vitamin C...

Spiritus sanctus, amen...

Different crafts on board

Purl one, stitch one...

What is this rusty old gun... ?

Master armourer

Checked, adjusted, repaired, rubbed the pistols, the shotguns, the blunderbusses and other firearms...

Master sail maker

On the fore-deck, responsible for the making and the mending of sail.

There was a jolly miller once
Lived on the river Dee
He work'd and sang from morn till night...

Butcher

Removed the cracklin' skin, deboned and cut off meat pieces for the staff.

*sshliiiiiic
sshliiiiiiick*

Baker

Kneaded the bread dough and made a few pastries for staff officers.

32

I'm watching him, that one !

The Steward's room

This was where the responsible for food and water retailing and rationing for the whole crew officiated, a figure extremely wooed for his generosity in giving extra food.

Easy up there, eeeeeeeasy !

The trimmer

Responsible for taking upstairs the goods stocked in the rooms and in the holds according to the needs but also responsible for the sharing out of the loads.

The naturalist *for discovery trips*

(most often being the doctor and surgeon at the same time, the apothecary...)
*He identified and collected when possible all the vegetal,
animal or mineral unknown species that they came accross
during stopovers in order to study them.*

Master caulker

*Kept the watertightness of the ship
on tracks and guarded against
any waterway at any time or place.*

> There's a hole in the bucket, dear Liza, dear Liza, There's a hole in the bucket, dear Liza, There's a hole.

> Derived from the latin word "sanguisuga" and from the hirudin family...

> By Jove ! I've been patching up the bulkward for the third time today...

Master carpenter

*Repaired or replaced
every damaged or broken pieces
of wood on the ship.*

33

> Don't play with fire !

> Darn waves ! Now I have a spot !

Master blacksmith

*Made or restored all the pieces
of metal used on the ship.*

> A glass of tafia, officer ?

Cartographer

*Responsible for drawing or clarify
the relief of the coastline covered during
travel in order to improve, piece by piece,
the marine maps.*

Cabin's boys

On the staff's exclusive service.

Ration for one week for 7 men

The master cook and his hands prepared 700 pints (665 l) of soup for one boiler. This was only possible in calm sea. In stress of weather, the fire risk was at such a point that the crew settled for a cold lunch.

	breakfast		lunch		supper	
Monday	biscuits 180 g each	water wine	salted beef 1,7 kg	water wine	peas 850 g	water wine
Tuesday		water wine	pig's foot 1,8 kg	water wine	beans 850 g	water wine
Wednesday		water wine	cod 850 g	water wine	fava beans 850 g	water wine
Thursday		water wine	salted bacon 1,2 kg	water wine	peas 850 g	water wine
Friday		water wine	cod 850 g	water wine	beans 850 g	water wine
Saturday		water wine	cod 850 g	water wine	fava beans 850 g	water wine
Sunday		water wine	salted bacon 1,2 kg	water wine	rice	water wine

The moth

The weevil

They were the faithful guests of the sailor's meal.

The bread

Shared out on Sundays to cheer up the sailors.

The tafia

A sugar cane eau-de-vie, the heartwarming drink.

The bells were rung with the quarter-deck bell just as many other events on board.

The can
(for the wine)
3 pints = 2,85 liters

The porringer
to contain
meat and fisch.

The small bowl
(basket)
for flatbreads.

The water-jar
to distribute water
that was put,
every morning,
at the forecastle
deck's entrance

An ox's horn with a
handle for the water
rations, capacity: 6 cl...

breakfast	summer 7:30, winter 8:00
lunch	1:30 PM
supper	summe 6:00, winter 5:30

dong

Vermin! Again!

The meals of the sailors

What a sissy!

The sailors, who were imposed rationing by groups of seven, improvised their meager daily bread, called "the dish", on the gun deck. They would gulp down the rancid food thoughtlessly and drink the water without smelling its rancid smell, with the only thought of stuffing their face to subsist whatever the price...

Captain,
your Cahors wine
is excellent!

Congratulations to
the cook, this fattened
chicken is heavenly!

In the staff officer's room, on the other hand, they didn't know about scarcity. Au menu, refined cooking, meat and live poultry coming from the stock yard, Great growths wine from Cahors or Bordeaux taken from personal wine cellars, daily bread, pastries. Rationing was not suitable...

The sailor

On the coasts of France, fishermen, boatmen, merchant seamen were counted according to the Royal law in effect in the 18th century. They owed one year of work in the King's navy every three or four years from the age of 14 and until they were 60 years old.

The boys

They went on board as soon as they were 10/12 years old.

Originally from the coast of Britanny, of Saintonge, Guyenne or from the Mediterranean seacoast , the sailor was a man experienced with the sea. He knew everything about seamanship.

He mastered maneuvers, he could do splices, the different knots were no secret for him, it was even a hobby when he had nothing else to do. He could strop, hit the pulleys, rig the shrouds and the shores, in fine or bad weather...

Coarse and sturdy, he had to to be well-fed and his bravery needed to be aroused. Superstitious, he knew how to identify a good captain.

Hygiene

No fresh water nor soap (still costly for that time), a permanent dampness, an unwanted promiscuity, exhausting chores, an inappropriate food : at sea, everything joined inevitably together to make of hygiene a rare commodity.
Fresh water, priceless, rationed out was only used to desalt food.
The laundry, rinced out with brackish water, didn't dry and caused painful skin infections...
The godsend of a hard rain and of heavy showers quickly cleaned out the minds of these customary torments..

GRAT GRAT GRAT

The loo...

The privy or the back head gratings of the head : one commode bench was placed on each board which makes 2 for 296 men.

Rather unfavorable to daydreaming, located at the extreme front of the ship and directly above the bowsprit, where the continuous waves ferociously lashed the stern, under the protective eye of the figurehead, a rudimentary platform was set up there for the needs of the cause, open to everyone. As you can easily imagine, the waves were useful and swift in erasing all the traces people left.

36

The officer

croac!

The officer, coming from a noble background, followed science teaching in arithmetic, in geometry and in mechanics.

At sea, under the command of his captain, he had to handle the riggings and to enforce discipline and authority without turning the watchful crew against him. He was above everything a soldier serving the navy and the king and had to make a carrier in hoping to appear among the finest flagships of the Crown...

Personal hygiene

His hygiene was much more elaborate. In his cabin, away from prying eyes, he could serenely attend his ablutions.
A wall fountain supplied with fresh water offered to everyone the possibility of a high-class toilette in there.
In relative privacy, and with his personal belongings, such as books, musical instruments, he could at will, forget for some time the harchness of the sea.

Bottles

Starboard : kept for the Captain's use.
Port : for the officers' use.
Placed on both sides at the back of the Hermione, in direct acces through the staff officers' room, this little closed place let the user to believe that there was much more comfort there.
Who knew, Maybe it was the scene of great reflections, or even historic decisions...

Toilet paper only appeared in the XIXth century in the form of paper bricks folded into pleats and of poor quality.
In the XVIIIth, ashore, relatively widespread papers were used as a substitute, while at sea, officers would probably opt for a linen or a hempen cloth...

Sleeping arrangements

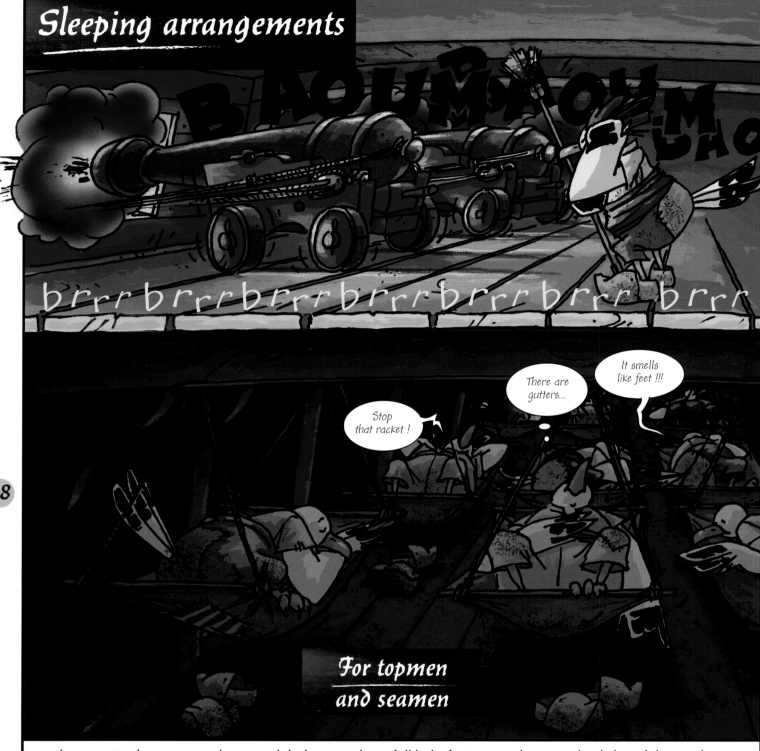

BAOUMAOH-M

brrr brrr brrr brrr brrr brrr brrr

Stop that racket !

There are gutters...

It smells like feet !!!

For topmen and seamen

In the pervasive dampness, in almost total darkness and in a full lack of privacy, each one, in the shelter of their rudimentary hammoc, enjoyed a refreshing sleep...

Watchmen

Seamen were divided into two categories : the men of the starboard watch and the men of the port watch.
While the men of the starboard watch were attending their business, the men of the port watch were at rest and vice versa.
Depending on the day or the night, each seaman had to go back to his post every 4 or 6 hours (to take his watch).
This strict work organisation in rotation avoided obstruction on the decks and regulated work and watch on the ship round-the-clock.
Space on board was extremely limited and each man had to respect his working area.

Discipline reigned on a frigate and mind the one who didn't follow orders.
The crew had to toe the line to safely sail such a large ship where space was scarce...

For the masters of the ship

The masters : surgeons, gunsmiths, carpenters, etc... Being better off than the others, they had single compartments on both side at the front of the orlop. They got on the ship with their personal belongings that they carefully kept in their living quarters and made sure that it didn't change hands...

The officers, the Captain

They had at their disposal bunks at the back of the orlop away from the major part of the crew.

He was the only one to own a cabin that was really isolated and to enjoy absolute privacy. He was free as he pleased to lapse into soft reveries. The only master on board after God and the only one with a genuine bedding...

Let's keep in mind that the Captain just as the officers had at their disposal devoted servants at their service and responsible for stewardship (the laundry, the dishes...)

Don't worry if it stings a little !

40

Tatooing

This practice, borrowed from the native peoples of the Pacific, was brought back by sailors fascinated by this decorative art. The technique spread all over the harbours of the world, here and there in shops and even directly in the street.
Aboard ships, seamen who could draw a little bit, practised this craft in return for a little profit...

Inks   A cloth   The needle

Music and dance

One-two-three !

Sea shanties

Fifteen Men on A Dead Man's Chest

Fifteen men on a dead man's chest
Yo ho ho and a bottle of rum
Drink and the devil had done for the rest
Yo ho ho and a bottle of rum.
The mate was fixed by the bosun's pike
The bosun brained with a marlinspike
And cookey's throat was marked belike
It had been gripped by fingers ten ;
And there they lay, all good dead men
Like break o'day in a boozing ken.
Yo ho ho and a bottle of rum.

A good jig to remove the knots in your stomach and to conjure spirits.

The jacks

A game of skills and of swiftness played during free time with little sheep bones (the carpus). The rule consisted in throwing in the air the only jack separated from the five others (the father, marked with one colour) and then grabbing one jack on the floor before it fell down again and catching it up.
The goal was to grab like this and successively 2 then 3 then the 4 jacks on the floor.

Punishment

Discipline

You don't mess with discipline aboard a ship with more than 300 men on it. Sanctions were regulated and subject to the Captain's decision, after a short deliberation. From a simple water privation, it could became worse and worse until capital punishment.

The ship's holdt

A hoisted red flag and gunfires to warn everyone around. The ship's hold was a torment generally pronounced in case of theft and that consisted in pushing the rogue one or twice off the sea from the main yard, arms, thighs and hands tied. The sailors of those times, most of them being bad swimmers hardly enjoyed this practice and the ones who were short of breath had to be careful...

117, 118...

Tied to the capstan

His hands tied and put in a humiliating position in front of everybody, the recalcitrant one was hit in series with a nipper.

Only 32 left...

Shackling

For the drunkards, the bruisers and other blasphemers, each one had his share of misery. On bread and water, confined for calls during an indefinite period of time. A painful sanction that they took really hard.

I have a hangman's knot in my stomach

41

Capital punishment

For the raiders, the arsonists or the murderers, punishment was heavy. From being marked with a hot iron (an anchor branded in hot iron) to being sentences to work on galleys and up to death penalty.

Don't move like that! You'll make me miss it...

I'd like to see you in my shoes, limb of the devil!

Stopovers were essential to the survival of the crew after many months at sea, with priority to change the fresh water that became rancid and foul and that caused serious digestive diseases among the seamen.

42

Stopovers

Ships that generally held stores for a duration of 6 months were confronted to rough conditions at sea that brought about many losses. Stopovers then became golden opportunities of refreshing supplies and also of respite for the seamen often mistreated aboard by heavy weather... They enabled them to satisfy their curiosity for distant and unexplored lands, an imposing sight of wild and lush vegetation and to set up accidental meetings with unknown animal species. But above everything, they gave them the opportunity to improve everyday fare in this genuine open air pantry. The top priority was to find a watering place, to fill up on water. Men went looking for a brook or a river to draw fresh water and fill up the hogsheads in necessary quantity for the crew. These islands gave plenty of wild vegetables, fresh fruit, animals to hunt and fish to catch... Everything that looked edible was picked, dug up or gathered. With all their heart and soul, seamen made the necessary supplies that could breathe new life into their stomachs. The naturalist at work indexed, sketched, completed his herbarium, filled up jars, cages and protective sackings* with all kinds of specimens, not any minute to waste !

Every man could taste, during a stopover, the nearly forgotten smells of the solid ground, and was quite free to come and go as he pleased through wide-open spaces... A pleasure, mutual to everyone, except for the confined ones.

*A protective sacking :
a braided wicket container used to preserve a plant and its roots into a clod so as to be transplanted.

Run for your life ! The unpredictable welcome of natives on an unknown land turned out to be most inhospitable, fleeing was then most often the only reasonable way out...

FLAP FLAP

Some other times when they were luckier, they were offered a little corner of paradise that they found difficult to leave...

Many legends were spread by word of mouth, from one ship to another, from one port to another, about these far-off lands, these paradise islands and these peoples from the other side of the world, as diverse and varied in the way they looked as in their customs, welcoming or aggressive, and who haunted the thoughts of the sea people. So many stories that have crossed the seas and the oceans and that have been passed on all over the years, all throughout History...

The return voyage

After all this time spent at sea, sailing to and from accross the four corners of the earth, returning to their home port was experienced as a relief. Most of them were burned out, sick, crippled, except for some tough fellows, these seamen emerged from a waking nightmare with their heads full of memories, good or bad, which would soon all throughout the world, in the dregs of eating houses, weave the legend of these adventurers of the seas and of the oceans... The eldest of them went through with the royal debt and as sea dogs, were beached in ports and in naval shipyards, haunting the back streets with their old wooly anecdotes for some small fry.
The youngest ones, the inexperienced ones, who had just been introduced to boarding, came back as men...
The holds were drained of their various specimens brought back from the antipodes, and the Hermione, in her turn, would end up in subgrade to be repaired in preparation for new adventures...

Lieutenant, would you please take my trunk down !

Yes, Sir !

Mother !

My son !

Ouch ! My stomach.

They don't look fresh...

Who was on this ship again ?

La Fayette, I guess, but watch your boat hook, zounds !

Warm thanks !

To those who let me free to do as I wanted,
and to the ones I directly or indirectly collaborated with
to complete this project successfully

The Hermione-La Fayette Association
www.hermione.com

Benedict Donnelly, president
Maryse Vital,
Isabelle Georget

and all the professionnals involved in the site.

I would like to give a special thought to our late Jean Thomas,
our historical advisor among the Association,
for his precious proofreading on the technical pages
and for his amused tolerance regarding the seagulls' sometimes inconventional tone...

45

Reproduit et achevé d'imprimer en Italie (Papergraf)

pour le compte de Gulf Stream Éditeur

Impasse du Forgeron, C.P. 910,

44806 Saint-Herblain cedex

Dépôt légal, 1re édition : avril 2011

www.gulfstream.fr